A bruised reed

One Christian's journey through depression

Phil Cottrell

EP BOOKS
Faverdale North
Darlington
DL3 0PH, England

web: http://www.epbooks.org

e-mail: sales@epbooks.org

EP Books are distributed in the USA by:
JPL Distribution
3741 Linden Avenue Southeast
Grand Rapids, MI 49548
E-mail: orders@jpldistribution.com
Tel: 877.683.6935

British Library Cataloguing in Publication Data available

ISBN 978–0–85234–998–4

"Simple, honest and gently written, this is an account of one Christian's journey through the experience of depression and anxiety, together with what he has learned along the painful path.

Easy on the ear, *A Bruised Reed* is likely to achieve its aims of helping fellow sufferers and giving understanding to Christians who themselves may not have been so afflicted.

Helpfully descriptive of the symptoms suffered by the author and beautifully strengthening in its focus on the Scriptures and the Saviour Himself, it encourages a realignment of thought, perseverance and a consideration of the Christian's great hope."

Simon Clarke, Pastor, Shepshed Word of Life Church

Chris

Thank you for your sincere care towards me and for encouraging me to write.

Phil

Contents

Introduction

This is a personal testimony of my experiences, and, I trust, lessons I have learned, concerning feelings and thoughts I have had regarding *depression* and *anxiety*. As far as I understand, these two intruders usually conspire together and this has certainly been the case with me.

I will not write about medication or professional help, since I am not medically trained and therefore not qualified to judge their effectiveness. Suffice to say that I see no reason to discount medical help. Since, as God provides professionals to treat our bodies, I presume that he provides the same for our minds. However, it is surely up to each Christian to decide for himself.

What I *do* feel able to write about is the Lord's wonderful love and care for one of his children who has suffered these two forms of disorder. I think we often shrink back from ailments of the mind, but as Christians we need to confront them in order to serve our God as we really desire.

I still get *depressed* and *anxious* but I can testify that our gracious Physician 'will keep [me] from all harm—he will watch over [my] life; the Lord will watch over [my] coming and going both now and for evermore' (Psalm 121:7–8).

There are three things I hope to do in these pages:

- to express thanks to the Lord for his healing.
- to be of help to my brothers and sisters who suffer from depression and anxiety.

- to give some understanding to Christians who are not so afflicted.

I wrote this introduction on 18 December 2010. Christmas is a time for rejoicing over the immeasurable gift of the Prince of Peace. Nevertheless, it is also one of the worst times of the year for depression. 'Let him who walks in the dark, who has no light, trust in the name of the LORD and rely upon his God' (Isaiah 50:10).

1

Unimaginably grim

The worst period of depression I have experienced was from October 2003 to August 2004, in which the most awful time was April and May 2004. In the deepest pain of mind, day after day, I hated each morning. I was glad when I could get to bed at night, but sleep was much shorter than I needed.

When I had recovered, I realized that I had suffered periods of depression for most of my adult life. I had not denied its presence, I simply did not recognize it for what it was. The mind is amazingly complex, and I would have needed to be a psychiatrist to explain all that was going on in my head.

I was 49 years old when my depression and anxiety were at their worst. Several problems led me to feel a loss of purpose and meaning in life. These are feelings that many people have at times and yet they manage to cope with them. I could not. The reason why came down to my having untrue, harmful thoughts and thus being overcome by life. How is this possible *for a Christian?*

If you suffer in this way then, before we go any further, let us consider two biblical examples of sufferers from depression, Elijah and Jeremiah, to prevent us from coming to the conclusion that we are an alien species!

First, Elijah:

'Elijah was afraid and ran for his life. When he came to Beersheba in Judah, he left his servant there, while he himself went a day's journey into the desert. He came to a broom tree, sat down under it and prayed that he might die. "I have had enough, LORD," he said. "Take my life; I am no better than my ancestors"' (1 Kings 19:3–4).

Here is a man of God, greatly used before and after this incident, in despair. Fear, exhaustion, feeling isolated and perhaps all sorts of other thoughts went through his mind to take him down into a pit of depression.

Second, Jeremiah:

'Cursed be the day I was born! May the day my mother bore me not be blessed! Cursed be the man who brought my father the news, who made him very glad, saying, "A child is born to you—a son!" … Why did I ever come out of the womb to see trouble

and sorrow and to end my days in shame?'
(Jeremiah 20:14–15, 18).

Jeremiah had the immense honour of
proclaiming the very words of God. He
knew an intimate fellowship with our Lord.
Yet, frail flesh and blood that he was, he
knew a time when he wished he hadn't been
born. We might be forgiven, as it were, for
not wanting to have a passage like this in
the Bible! But God has given it to us that we
may learn from it. Jeremiah was in a black
abyss but our Lord did not forsake him.
Our Father never abandons his children.
There are no hopeless cases in his sight!

2

'It was good for me to be afflicted'

One of the most distressing things about a deep depression is a profound feeling of confusion and disorientation. Day after day your mind struggles to make sense of things. I felt like a man drowning in the sea, groping to lay hold of the lifebelt that was *just* out of reach.

As we come to look later at our Saviour's wonderful, masterful means of helping someone who is depressed, it may be good to pause and ask, 'What is the purpose in allowing someone to go through such dark times?' A person in such distress thinks (wrongly) that he is useless, hopeless and unlovable. He asks himself, 'What good can *possibly* come from such a situation?'

The best answer I can give, from personal experience, is the priceless gift of having been brought, albeit 'kicking and screaming', into a closer relationship with the Lord Jesus. 'It was good for me to be afflicted so that I might learn your decrees' (Psalm 119:71). As this verse says, our help comes from the Scriptures, and I would suggest the key word is 'learn'. We all need the heart and mind of our Lord. As the apostle Paul says: 'Your attitude should be the same as that of Christ Jesus: who, being in very nature God, did not consider equality with God something to be grasped, but made himself nothing, taking the very nature of a servant, being made in human likeness. And being found in appearance

as a man, he humbled himself and became
obedient to death—even death on a cross!'
(Philippians 2:5–8).

Our wonderful Lord has shown us
how to live. He calls us to service and
obedience. Here is a seeming paradox:
that at a time when a person feels a lack
of self-worth, he is in danger from pride.
I think we can all struggle with pride, but
depression especially feeds self-pity, and
self-centredness is one of the characteristics
of pride. Let us *all* recognize the weakness
in our nature when we are feeling low.

But, before we allow this to send us into
a downward spiral of guilt and helplessness
(the very opposite of my intention!), we
need to be reminded of the biblical truth
God has given to us about himself—'Who
is a God like you, who pardons sin and
forgives the transgression of the remnant
of his inheritance? You do not stay angry
for ever but delight to show mercy. You
will again have compassion on us; you will
tread our sins underfoot and hurl all our

iniquities into the depths of the sea. You will be true to Jacob, and show mercy to Abraham, as you pledged on oath to our fathers in days long ago' (Micah 7:18–20).

Jesus, during his earthly ministry, had many of the experiences that grieve the human heart. He knew persecution, violence, insults, hatred, betrayal, isolation, disappointment, exhaustion, extreme hunger and thirst, mourning and forsakenness. 'He was despised and rejected by men, a man of sorrows and familiar with suffering' (Isaiah 53:3). Yet, through all the pain of living in this fallen world, experiencing grief deeper than we know because he is the Son of God, he had great joy and peace.

If we are not careful, life can seem an unremitting struggle and a load of care. Is this not a recipe for depression? Once again, I think we need to lay hold of the command of Scripture and *'learn'* from our Lord—'Come to me, all you who are weary and burdened, and I will give you rest. Take

my yoke upon you and learn from me, for I
am gentle and humble in heart, and you will
find rest for your souls. For my yoke is easy
and my burden is light' (Matthew 11:28–30).

3

Bad signs

There are signs that indicate a person is depressed, which I am sure are well known to many people. Yet, they are worth stating, to help us see the symptoms and so do battle with this affliction.

There can be a 'heaviness' about everything. Every little thing seems a matter of life and death, yet, in reality, how few situations in life fall into that category! It can become difficult to make even simple decisions, worrying over trifles, so that making progress is like walking through treacle.

Another major symptom is irritability. It is so arduous for someone who is depressed to think clearly. Noise, delays, unexpected tasks and unhelpful people appear as major hurdles to be overcome, when the person has barely enough energy to get through the day.

The problems and difficulties of *my* life can seem so much worse than other people's. I see other people, other Christians, apparently sailing calmly through life's waters and this can create a sort of 'martyr' mentality—I am a poor victim of circumstances beyond my control! A prison does not necessarily have metal bars. Self-preoccupation is, I believe, a problem we *all* battle with. In my experience, it is one of the hardest things to overcome, and this has certainly been the case when I have been depressed. I have sometimes felt as though the whole universe revolves around *me*. We will look at 'self-forgetfulness' later, but suffice to say that it is a wonderful balm for a troubled mind, given to us by a gracious Saviour.

So then, even Christians can come to a position where they ask, 'What's the point?' If life, even the Christian life, is just one source of pain after another, where is the purpose in it all?

I used to imagine Christians who never seemed to experience depression and anxiety, shaking their heads in disbelief at such thoughts. I thought they must be horrified at my erroneous thinking. And that of course was my problem in a nutshell—*such thinking is in error.* (Incidentally other Christians did not judge me like I imagined. I have since learned that they were concerned about and were praying for me).

'O LORD, you have searched me and you know me. You know when I rise; you perceive my thoughts from afar.

You discern my going out and my lying
down. You are familiar with all my ways.
Before a word is on my tongue you know it
completely, O Lord' (Psalm 139:1–4).

'We are the clay, you are the potter; we
are all the work of your hand' (Isaiah 64:8).
The God we worship and serve, who has
revealed himself in the person of the Lord
Jesus Christ, knows all things, and that
includes how our minds work. His desire,
as our loving Father, is that we know
his peace. He has the power to heal any
depression and he will lovingly help us to
overcome this debilitating condition.

4

The sky falling In

A major problem that has fuelled my depression has been anticipating the worst. All of us need to remind ourselves that we have a Father who loves us very much, and it grieves him to see his children worried. Has not Jesus said: 'Look at the birds of the air; they do not sow or reap or store away in barns, and yet your heavenly Father feeds them. Are you not much more valuable than they?' (Matthew 6:26).

'See how the lilies of the field grow. They do not labour or spin. Yet I tell you that not even Solomon in all his splendour was dressed like one of these' (Matthew 6:28–29).

How are we to combat worry? 'So do not worry, saying, "What shall we eat?" or "What shall we drink?" or "What shall we wear?" For the pagans run after all these things, and your heavenly Father knows that you need them. *But seek first his kingdom and his righteousness, and all these things will be given to you as well'* (Matthew 6:31–33). If I am taken up with the Lord Jesus, and how to honour, serve, and glorify him, everything else falls into place.

What is 'worry'? It is the fruitless and draining exercise of trying to dot every 'i' and cross every 't' for all the *potential* eventualities that may arise. Inevitably, the mind turns to the negative, the worst possible (and, often, impossible!) outcome. We must rest in his loving care: 'Trust in the LORD with all your heart and lean not on your own understanding; in all your ways acknowledge him, and he will make your paths straight' (Proverbs 3:5–6).

Just trusting the Lord and not getting anxious is much easier said than done. But, of course, he knows this! I must ask him to help me to take him at his word, and remind myself again and again that I am precious in his sight.

The air we breathe is given to us by God. The sky above us is evidence of our Lord's creative power and of his provision for mankind, whom he has made. But what if the sky were to fall in on top of me? What would I do then? This sounds absurd, doesn't it? I have put questions like this to myself in the past deliberately to show myself how laughable anxiety can be. This has been a means of giving myself a good talking to. I am a *rational* being, and the ability to reason logically reflects the image of the God who made me. Faith may *seem* to contradict reason, but the truth is it *transcends* reason.

Hebrews chapter 11 speaks of those who lived 'by faith' and so pleased God. As was quoted in the introduction to this journey, 'Let him who walks in the dark, who has no light, trust in the name of the LORD and rely upon his God' (Isaiah 50:10).

5

Walking on eggshells

One of the problems a depressed person has is that he feels *vulnerable*. I know that when I have felt down, silly little things that people have said or done, and what they have *not* said or done, have made me feel hurt. If people I come into contact with pick up on this, my oversensitivity can make them feel so wary of upsetting me that they act as if they are walking on eggshells. A word out of place and Phil will break into pieces! Much of this vulnerability which I have felt has come from thoughts such as 'I am worthless. I can't do much, and what I can do doesn't make a difference to anyone.' It has been a great comfort for me to be reminded that 'worthless' and 'useless' are not *true* descriptions regarding *any* of God's children: they are not *biblical.*

'May they be brought to complete unity to let the world know that you sent me and have loved them even as you have loved me?' (John 17:23). God the Father loves us in the same way, to the same extent, that he loves his Son, because we are in Christ. Within the Godhead is a pure, perfect love, and this is how *we* are loved. No loving father would tell his child that they are worthless and useless, and it would grieve him deeply if his child thought that of himself. How much more so would such thoughts grieve a holy God?

I think it is very helpful to remember that pride and self-respect are not the same thing. Pride is self-deceit and falsehood, whereas self-respect is a true statement of one's intrinsic value in God's sight. We all need to live in the light of what God's Word says about us.

6

Guilty as charged, M'lord

As Christians, we have 'good news' to proclaim to guilty sinners. Let *us* not lose sight of the mercy *we* have received. When I feel depressed, feelings of guilt can be a major problem. I say to myself, 'I have let myself down, I have let other people down, and worst of all I have let my Lord down.' Depression makes a person especially vulnerable to guilt. What then am

I to do? Depression and anxiety are not *sins* (although they may become sinful if not properly dealt with) The problem is centred around our thoughts. If we constantly see our mental problems as sin, this view will be like a huge weight on our backs. It is a lot harder to climb up steps carrying a heavy burden!

Yes, you are a sinner, just like I am, and so you recognise sin in your life. Like me, you try to keep 'short accounts' with your God, confessing your sins, remembering that 'the blood of Jesus, his Son, purifies [me] from all sin' (1 John 1:7). That little word 'all' is immensely important. I must totally reject the lie that a certain sin, or sins, are unforgivable in our Lord's sight— not just 'recent' sin, but also sin from the past, perhaps even from years ago. I can rake up sin, thinking about all my failure in meticulous detail. But the sin has been forgiven in God's sight, and I must tell myself this, again and again, if necessary.

Our Lord Jesus is love personified. When

he walked the earth, all his dealings with people were loving, even with those who hated him. God the Father and God the Son are one, and so, of course, our Father in heaven has the same pure, perfect love for us as Jesus. In 1 Corinthians 13, Paul tells us what love is, and, if we substitute 'sin' for 'wrongs', then we have a wonderful, joyous answer to our guilty thoughts—'[love] keeps no record of wrongs' (1 Corinthians 13:5).

7

'Hope in God'

Depression can make a person feel as though he has no future. I remember when I was really ill, the feeling of hopelessness became so bad it made me despair. Each day lacked meaning and purpose, and the thought of tomorrow seemed to beckon more of the same. In Ecclesiastes we find such thoughts expressed repeatedly. What was Solomon's problem? In essence, he left God out of the picture.

Our Father does not abandon his children. With him, there are no 'hopeless cases'. 'With God all things are possible' (Matthew 19:26). I must continually look to *the Lord,* and what I can be, and do, *through him.* God posed the question, 'Is anything too hard for the LORD?' (Genesis 18:14), and Jeremiah gives us the answer—'Ah, Sovereign LORD, you have made the heavens and the earth by your great power and outstretched arm. Nothing is too hard for you' (Jeremiah 32:17). He has made us. He knows all about our bodies, our feelings, our emotions, and our minds. Through all my doubts and fears, confusion and perplexity, I know that my Father looks upon me with love. 'He delights to show mercy' (Micah 7:18).

We have a Saviour who loves us very much, a Saviour who knew that the cross lay before him and knew the suffering of this life. As the Bible says, 'For we do not have a high priest who is unable to sympathise with our weaknesses, but we have one who has been tempted in every way, just as we are—yet was without sin. Let us then approach the throne of grace with confidence, so that we may receive mercy and find grace to help us in our time of need' (Hebrews 4:15–16).

I do not know what suffering you are experiencing, nor can I see inside your heart and mind—*but God can.* When I go through a period of depression, I need to give myself a good talking to. I cannot do this for you, nor you for me. *Three times,* God's Word says to us, 'Why are you downcast, O my soul? Why so disturbed within me?' As the psalmist speaks to himself, *so must we.* And what was the answer? *'Put your hope in God,* for I will yet praise him, my Saviour and my God' (Psalm 42:5 and 11 and Psalm 43:5).

8

A sacred song

Many people have memories of hurtful and traumatic experiences. These memories may be so painful that a person remains a psychological and emotional casualty. If this is true for me as a Christian, how am I to serve the Lord with these painful thoughts lodged deep in my mind? Undoubtedly, depression and anxiety are possible consequences, so—how do I handle this?

God *can* and *does* most wonderfully heal a wounded mind. If we seek his help, our loving Father will minister to us through the Holy Spirit. He is the author of the Scriptures and will enlighten us through them, putting thoughts of our Lord Jesus in the place of harmful thoughts. Does this sound naïve, simplistic or just plain unreal? Then let us ask this question, 'For what purpose has God given us the Bible, if not in part to set our thinking right?'

My experience, which I am sure is far from unique, is that at times when I feel anxious or depressed, reading the Bible can be hard going. I may *read* the words, but do I take them in? The only answer I have is to persevere, praying for the Lord's help, both before I read and as I read. Like any healing process, it takes time.

What assurances do we have from God's Word itself that he will help us to serve him through meditating upon the Scriptures? I think Psalm 119 is most helpful to us in this respect. Here are a few verses from this psalm for us to consider:

v 11—'I have hidden your word in my heart that I might not sin against you.'

v 18—'Open my eyes that I may see wonderful things in your law.'

v 28—'My soul is weary with sorrow; strengthen me according to your word.'

v 73—'Your hands made me and formed me; give me understanding to learn your commands.'

v 89—'Your word, O Lord, is eternal; it stands firm in the heavens.'

v 91—'Your laws endure to this day, for all things serve you.'

v 105—'Your word is a lamp to my feet and a light for my path.'

v 130—'The unfolding of your words gives light; it gives understanding to the simple.'

v 133—'Direct my footsteps according to your word; let no sin rule over me.'

v 143—'Trouble and distress have come

upon me, but your commands are my delight.'

v 153—'Look upon my suffering and deliver me, for I have not forgotten your law.'

v 160—'All your words are true; all your righteous laws are eternal.'

v 165—'Great peace have they who love your law, and nothing can make them stumble.'

9

The blame game

Have you noticed how easy it is to point the finger at the deficiencies of others, whilst excusing one's own? It is in the nature of our sinful hearts to do this. Specifically, of course, it is our pride which sees the faults in others but chooses to be blind to our own.

Jesus said, 'Why do you look at the speck of sawdust in your brother's eye and pay no attention to the plank in your own eye?

How can you say to your brother, "Let me take the speck out of your eye," when all the time there is a plank in your own eye? You hypocrite, first take the plank out of your own eye, and then you will see clearly to remove the speck from your brother's eye' (Matthew 7:3–5).

Harsh, even resentful thoughts about people are the product of a mind confused and perplexed, looking to blame *anyone* for his problems other than himself. When such thoughts arise, we need to ask the Lord to take them away, in the assurance that he will do so.

10

Help is at hand

Each Christian that lives, regardless of his mental well-being, is limited in the thoughts that he has. Like the margins on a page, his thoughts fall within certain parameters. If he is to see differently (which he *must* if suffering from depression), he needs help from other Christians. Whatever professional help you get, you are still part of the body of Christ. 'The eye cannot say to the hand, "I don't need you!" And the head cannot say to the feet, "I don't need you!" On the contrary, those parts of the body that seem to be weaker are indispensable, and the parts that we think are less honourable we treat with special honour' (1 Corinthians 12:21–23).

Sometimes when I feel down, my prevailing thought is that I am pretty useless, not much good to anyone. But what does *God* say about me? 'Those parts of the body that seem to be weaker are *indispensable*.' There are two aspects to this: *I* need to grasp that I am vital to the well-being of the church, and the *church* needs to grasp that I am vital to them. Take heart! You are precious to the Lord Jesus.

'God has combined the members of the body and has given greater honour to the parts that lacked it, so that there should be no division in the body, but that its parts should have equal concern for each other. If one part suffers, every part suffers with it; if one part is honoured, every part rejoices with it' (1 Corinthians 12:24–26).

When you know that a Christian is suffering, do you in turn feel his pain? If he is depressed and anxious, do you comfort him in any way you can, and cry out to your Father for healing for him? When I ask myself this question, I feel woefully lacking. But the Lord has promised to forgive my sin if I confess it to him. If I recognize my need, that I *must* help my brother in his distress, God has *also* promised to help me. 'Ask and it will be given to you; seek and you will find; knock and the door will be opened to you. For everyone who asks receives; he who seeks finds; and to him who knocks, the door will be opened. Which of you, if his son asks for bread, will give him a stone? Or if he asks for a fish, will give him a snake? If you, then, though you are evil, know how to give good gifts to your children, how much more will your Father in heaven give good gifts to those who ask him! So in everything, do to others what you would have them do to you, for this sums up the Law and the Prophets' (Matthew 7:7–12).

Sometimes, a major problem for me when I am depressed is the tendency to 'close in' on myself. That is, to physically isolate myself from other Christians. I excuse myself, thinking, 'They don't understand; they can't really help; it's just too hard to be interested in them at the moment.' In my experience, there is really only one answer to this problem—*make yourself* spend time with other Christians, either in a group or one-to-one. I have found both to be helpful.

Remember, you need help, and *you cannot do it alone.* You may ask, 'What blessing am I to *them? How* can *they* be blessed in the company of someone who struggles to raise a smile, and whose thoughts in conversation seem to go off at a tangent?' Well, one immense blessing is that you will provide an opportunity for them to be obedient to God's Word—'Carry each other's burdens, and in this way you will fulfill the law of Christ' (Galatians 6:2).

11

'... For one of the least ...'

We all have a need to feel loved. It is a basic part of what makes us human. Our Lord Jesus found love at the home of Lazarus, Mary and Martha. The disciples were surely a source of love for him; in Gethsemane he sought their company. He is described as 'a man of sorrows, and familiar with suffering' (Isaiah 53:3). This follows on from the same verse which tells us 'He was despised and rejected by men.' In his humanity, did not our Saviour know the awfulness of being abandoned by people?

Depression is an illness of the mind. In its grip, a person can feel very alone, separated from people, even though there may be plenty of people around. I remember an occasion when I felt particularly low, and a dear brother in the Lord showed that he cared about me, just from a smile and a handshake. Never underestimate the blessing that can come from showing that you care for a brother or sister. Also, let us not forget whom we serve. 'The King will reply, "I tell you the truth, whatever you did for one of the least of these brothers of mine, you did for me"' (Matthew 25:40).

In showing love to someone who is depressed, we need two qualities above all—patience and gentleness. We need patience, because helping a fellow Christian out of the blackness he is in will almost certainly take a long period. Are we prepared to give of our time? Am I willing to bear with his distress, repeating the comfort of the Scriptures again and again? We need gentleness, because a depressed person can feel incredibly fragile. Our presence needs to be a source of comfort, a place where burdens and sorrows can be offloaded.

Love, patience and gentleness are all fruit of the Spirit. Let us seek and pray for these beautiful qualities, that we may be able to give comfort. 'A friend loves at all times, and a brother is born for adversity' (Proverbs 17:17).

12

An alternative place to be

Sometimes people will ask, 'Where are you spiritually?' and 'How is your walk with the Lord?' As Christians, so far as our day-to-day lives are concerned, we can be in close fellowship with the Lord Jesus, or we can be far from him. Along with our bodies, the health of our hearts and minds are intimately bound together, shaping our well-being. I find it easy to think in terms of absolutes as a Christian. There are times when I am on a mountain-top, and there are times when I am in a deep valley. The reality is that most of the time I am in neither place, but traversing along a rugged path, hoping by God's grace to know him better. How does this apply to depression?

There is all the difference in the world between *'feeling'* depressed and *'being'* depressed. This is not just playing with words. If you *feel* depressed you can lift yourself up, give yourself a good talking-to and move into the daylight. If you *are* depressed, *this is the place you are in,* a state of gloom which is *much* harder to get out of. Two conditions, yet one vital lesson. It is imperative to address depression *before* it envelops you.

What strategy can I adopt to prevent depression and anxiety from taking hold? As always, the answer lies in God's Word. In the next three chapters we shall look at three biblical themes which are invaluable to us. 'You will keep him in perfect peace whose mind is stayed on you, because he trusts in you' (Isaiah 26:3, New King James Version).

13

'Be thankful'
—*a biblical command*

It can be easy to be taken up with our needs, urgent and essential as they may be, and neglect thanksgiving.

Or, at least, that has been my experience. I think this can be the case especially when battling depression. Our minds get preoccupied with problems and we plead for help from our heavenly Father, all too aware of our inadequacies, and the blessings we have already received from him are overlooked. 'Let the peace of Christ rule in your hearts, since as members of one body you were called to peace. And be thankful. Let the word of Christ dwell in you richly as you teach and admonish one another with all wisdom, and as you sing psalms, hymns and spiritual songs with gratitude in your hearts to God. And whatever you do, whether in word or deed, do it all in the name of the Lord Jesus, giving thanks to God the Father through him' (Colossians 3:15–17).

One thing I have found to be really helpful is deliberately to spend time in prayer which is 'request free'—not asking for *anything*, but simply thanking the Lord for his gifts. Psalm 103 is a great help for this. 'Praise the LORD, O my soul; all my inmost being, praise his holy name. Praise the LORD, O my soul, and forget not all his benefits—who forgives all your sins and heals all your diseases, who redeems your life from the pit and crowns you with love and compassion, who satisfies your desires with good things so that your youth is renewed like the eagle's' (Psalm 103:1–5). *Whatever* our circumstances, however troubled our thoughts may be, we have things which, as this psalm tells us, we can *always* thank God for. Here are some of them, based on this psalm:

Forgiveness (v 3):	Eternally, in the Lord Jesus.
Healing (v 3):	Restoration of body, mind and spirit
Love (v 4):	From the God who 'is love'
Satisfaction (v 5):	The fulfilment of Godly desires
Justice (v 6):	Our God knows and 'will repay'
Revelation (v 7):	His Word, revealing the Lord Jesus
Grace (v 8):	He shows us undeserved kindness
Mercy (vv 10–12):	in which 'He delights'
Pity (vv 13–18):	He knows our weakness

His Sovereignty (v 19):	He is Lord: 'even the wind and waves obey Him'
The rightness of praise (vv 20–22):	He commands and receives praise!

The God whom we worship and serve is eternal—without beginning, without end, *unchanging*. Unlike us, he is *always* loving, holy and faithful and so it is *always* good to thank him for all he has done and continues to do for us. 'Jesus Christ is the same yesterday, today and forever' (Hebrews 13:8). 'Through Jesus, therefore, let us continually offer to God a sacrifice of praise—the fruit of lips that confess his name' (Hebrews 13:15).

We should also remember to thank our Father for other things he blesses us with: things which come and go, but which he nevertheless provides for us out of his loving care. Here are just a few: food, drink, home, family, friends, work, fellowship, Christian books and the countryside. Not all of us may know all of these gifts, but surely we have opportunity to give thanks for at least some of them.

It is the eternal *character* of our God, Father, Son and Holy Spirit, which is the rock on which we stand 'Praise the LORD, O my soul. O LORD my God, you are very great; you are clothed with splendour and majesty. He wraps himself in light as with a garment' (Psalm 104:1–2).

14

'Let us fix our eyes on Jesus ...'
—a biblical imperative

To be preoccupied with *self,* 'me/myself/I', fuels depression. And when a person is depressed, self-preoccupation can become a habit. At times when I have felt depressed, my thinking has been such that it was as if the whole world revolved around me. That is not only perverse, it is also harmful, potentially extremely harmful. How can this cycle of self-centredness be broken?

Our thoughts do not exist in a vacuum. If I am to take my thoughts away from myself, I must put something in their place. Or, better and more accurately, I must put *someone* in their place. 'Let us fix our eyes on Jesus, the author and perfecter of our faith, who for the joy set before him endured the cross, scorning its shame, and sat down at the right hand of the throne of God' (Hebrews 12:2). If our eyes and our thoughts are centred on the Lord, they will not be upon ourselves. He has given us the precious gift of faith to believe in him, laid down his life for us, and is enthroned in heaven—Lord of lords and King of kings. Should we not be preoccupied with how to serve him and our brothers and sisters?

Hebrews 12:1 says, 'let us throw off everything that hinders and the sin that so easily entangles' and 12:3 says, 'so that you will not grow weary and lose heart.' Allowing depression and anxiety to take hold of us will certainly wear us down and make our hearts feel like lead weights. The alternative is to have hearts and minds fixed on the Lord Jesus, in obedience to his Word.

A quality that is priceless in the struggle against depression and anxiety is *'self-forgetfulness'*. If we *meditate* upon the work and person of the Lord Jesus, we will forget ourselves and so the thoughts that harm us will disappear, like a bucket of water disappears in the vastness of the ocean.

We live by faith, and I quote again a verse that has really helped me: 'Let him who walks in the dark, who has no light, trust in the name of the LORD and rely upon his God' (Isaiah 50:10). What has also been a great help to me is having a number of Scripture passages, specifically concerning our Saviour, typed out in a folder. These are at hand for me to read regularly, and I give this as a suggestion for you.

Whatever our routine and timetable for reading God's Word, we all have a need to *encounter* Jesus in the pages of Scripture, through the enabling of the Holy Spirit.

15

'Our citizenship is in Heaven'
—a biblical promise

There are some thoughts which feed depression. Do you sometimes feel that life is not what it was meant to be? You sort one problem out, and another one comes along to take its place. Or troubles arrive one upon another so fast that you cannot figure out which to try and deal with first? Life can be so *frustrating,* nothing is as it should be.

Actually, there is a real danger in that last phrase. What we *should* say is that sometimes nothing is as *we* think it should be. There is a great mystery here, but ultimately, in the sovereign purposes of Almighty God, there is no other way that life upon earth *could* be. He is in control of everything: 'I make known the end from the beginning, from ancient times, what is still to come. I say: My purpose will stand, and I will do all that I please' (Isaiah 46:10).

Nevertheless, amidst the love, joy and peace with which our loving Father blesses us, there is also pain, sorrow, fear and trouble. This is hardly a revelation! Satan and the powers of darkness bring misery into people's lives—the result of the Fall. Even though I know all this, and I trust in my God's loving care, deep down in my soul there exists a longing for something *better.* And, of course, *there will be!* 'But our citizenship is in heaven. And we eagerly await a Saviour from there, the Lord Jesus Christ' (Philippians 3:20).

In heaven we will be rid of the presence of sin forever, and so there will be no more suffering. John has told us what will happen, and these future events are certain, because they are the promises of our risen Lord Jesus. 'Then I saw a new heaven and a new earth, for the first heaven and the first earth had passed away, and there was no longer any sea. I saw the Holy City, the new Jerusalem, coming down out of heaven from God, prepared as a bride beautifully dressed for her husband: And I heard a loud voice from the throne saying, "Now the dwelling of God is with men, and he will live with them. They will be his people, and God himself will be with them and be their God. He will wipe every tear from their eyes. There will be no more death or mourning or crying or pain, for the old order of things has passed away"' (Revelation 21:1–4).

When the troubles of this life hang

over our minds like a thick fog, and we just cannot see our way forward, we need to meditate upon heaven. The fog will lift eventually, in the light of a beautiful future. Depression makes me think upon circumstances, and thinking upon distressing circumstances leads me to feel depressed! Thoughts of heaven are a great help. This is *not* escapism, heaven is a *reality* for all God's people. One day, I will be in the very presence of my wonderful Lord Jesus; immersed in his love, I will serve and praise him perfectly for all eternity. 'You have made known to me the path of life; you will fill me with joy in your presence, with eternal pleasures at your right hand' (Psalm 16:11).

16

'... of the same family'

As I have read these pages, in which I have tried to come to grips with the subjects of depression and anxiety, it struck me how often I used the word 'help'. This leads my thoughts to a favourite psalm of mine, quoted in the introduction. Here are two more verses from it, which wonderfully answer a question that troubled minds ask: 'I lift up my eyes to the hills—where does my help come from? My help comes from the LORD, the Maker of heaven and earth' (Psalm 121:1–2).

What do I, and many of my brothers and sisters, need help *with?* We struggle with apprehension about the future, over-concern about what people think or say about us, debilitating thoughts of inadequacy, worry, recurring feelings of guilt and failure, and other ways to describe *fear*. God knows all about us. His Son has shared our humanity in all respects, except sin. 'Both the one who makes men holy and those who are made holy are of the same family. So Jesus is not ashamed to call them brothers' (Hebrews 2:11). Our loving Father does not want us to be afraid, *and has said so in his Word.* Again and again I have needed to lay hold of a promise in Isaiah, and I hope you will too: 'For I am the LORD, your God, who takes hold of your right hand and says to you, do not fear; I will help you' (Isaiah 41:13).

17

One day at a time

Coping with depression, and coming through the worst it can do, is often a slow process—sometimes a *painfully* slow process. This has certainly been my experience. When days with this intruder persist, it can be easy to say, 'When will this *ever* end?'

I don't think patience comes easily to any of us. When a person feels depressed, he needs to work through it, bit by bit. It is clear from Scripture that patience is something we need to work at: 'Brothers, as an example of patience in the face of suffering, take the prophets who spoke in the name of the Lord. As you know, we consider blessed those who have persevered. You have heard of Job's perseverance and have seen what the Lord finally brought about. The Lord is full of compassion and mercy' (James 5:10–11).

How many days can you live at a time? Only one! We can so easily burden *today* with the problems of *tomorrow*. We read in God's Word of Christians who lived *each* day to the full, led by the Holy Spirit. This surely is what we desire for ourselves. Some of our brothers and sisters in the early church must have wrestled with depression and anxiety, but nevertheless glorified the Lord: 'They devoted themselves to the apostles' teaching and the fellowship, to the breaking of bread and to prayer' (Acts 2:42).

I love that word 'devoted'. They gave their whole hearts, minds and wills to these activities, as a husband and wife should be *devoted* to each other. The Christians in Acts 2 knew that Jesus loved them: 'For I am convinced that neither death nor life, neither angels nor demons, neither the present nor the future, nor any powers, neither height nor depth, nor anything else in all creation, will be able to separate us from the love of God that is in Christ Jesus our Lord' (Romans 8:38–39).

18

The wrong question

I hope this description of my journey has been a help to you if you suffer from depression and anxiety. I hope it has helped you even if you *do not,* so that you can better comfort someone who is so afflicted.

There is, I am sure, much more that can be said about depression and anxiety, but this is how it has been for me. If this little book is a help to *one* of my brothers or sisters, I will be thankful to the Lord. Our

God knows all things, including what goes on in our minds. Ultimately, it is *he* who helps, heals and restores.

As I said in the introduction, I am not medically trained, so I am not qualified to write about the diagnosis or treatment of mental illness. One thing I *am* 'qualified' to write about is the love, grace, patience and gentleness of our heavenly Father and his Son, the Lord Jesus Christ—and that is what I have tried to do. As is written of our Lord Jesus, 'A bruised reed he will not break' (Isaiah 42:3).

A question that I have asked many times is, 'What is my life all about?' Minds that are in pain, confused and perplexed, ask such questions. But this is the *wrong* question. It is not, '*what* is it all about?' It is '*who* is it all about?'

Lives, my life and yours, have one purpose, which is to serve and glorify the Lord Jesus: 'You are not your own; you were bought at a price' (1 Corinthians 6:19–20). Whether our minds are well or unwell, the best thoughts we can have are centred upon our Saviour. If we meditate upon the person and work of God's Son, peace of mind will not be far away. 'He is the image of the invisible God, the firstborn over all creation. For by him all things were created: things in heaven and on earth, visible and invisible, whether thrones or powers or rulers or authorities; all things were created by him and for him. He is before all things, and in him all things hold together. And he is the head of the body, the church; he is the beginning and the firstborn from among the dead, so that in everything he might have the supremacy' (Colossians 1:15–18).